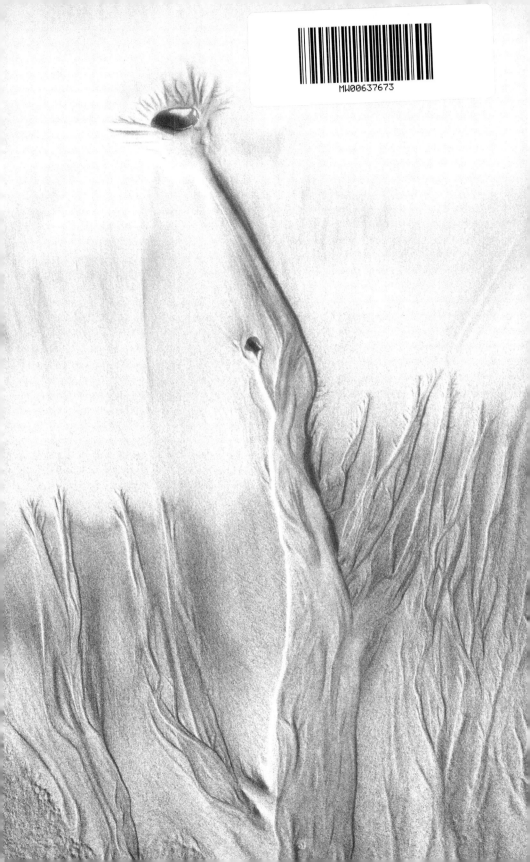

ea's e

Scott Metz

ea's e

ISBN 978-1-947271-95-1

Red Moon Press
PO Box 2461
Winchester VA
22604-1661 USA
www.redmoonpress.com

Cover photograph
and all section photographs
by Masako Metz

Cover design by Jason Amey & Scott Metz

Back cover: "sustenantce" (2022) by Scott Metz

first printing

For Masako & Phoenix

"Is it a long poem if you look at it long enough?"

Robert Grenier

BOMB #132

"It is as if time stopped and flowed
with no regularity; in some cases,
time seems to have flowed backwards."

Makoto Ueda

from The Principles of Classical Japanese Literature

ea's e

awkward. Laughter in
the green. Room
        of the Anthropocene

draft

of the sea

the

beginning

of

the   pine

's   thought

s

bird
 notes

the
 sun

  god's
name

winds of Venus
    there's a chance
  she's asleep

may
be
rain

may
be
me

a cricket's voice
    from deep inside
  Jupiter's eye

sun

wire

tap

ping

us

a god that never noticed me before the peony shadow

getting
blood

out
of a
stone

garden

a piece of the stone god in its shadow

—the
so. Und
of
           the ear. Th
             , leaving
     the l
ea. F

light in
the light
winter rain

night   bird
         notes
        that
could

fill

   the
      sun

full on   associations i regurgitate the moon

snow

falling

i n   to

a

question

of

light

borrowed
woods. add
ed

color.
fiction go
es.
without

saying

spring
tones
rent
a
night
elevator

if in doubt cherry blossoms

while the lilacs bloomed
a revolution
        came and went

insect too
close to
home

another prairie lost in a butterfly

fire
fly

      there
's
        a   n

      other

    time

      machine

the
wind's   carved
the
leaf   into a
                          forest

        the
        wind's   carved

                                            the
                                            leaf

        in

        to

        a
        forest

shrine for a god the bullet train begins to slow

this
leaf's
ear

marked

the
sun

the city looks gift wrapped underground news

                    hungry

                              spar
                              row
                              s
                bring

            me
            in
                              to the

                light

                              rain

always

      fog

              and

              or

      smoke

              pass

              ing

              thru

always

      the

      house

always

              UNDER

              CONSTRUCTION

between birds an exaggeration of stairs and doors

a dead beetle
brightly reflecting
the underworld

anger forms the year enters puberty doors to gift shops

siren by siren
gull by gull in
visible city

she left behind
an empty perfume bottle
the voice of frogs

our silence fogs the window the city inside us

how we've. grown.
intimate. w the. sea
the. last. few. river. teeth.

the weight of a crow
perched naked
on a semi-colon

sometimes the wind lifts up its wing to read

a view

                    branch   pivot
                         s

    on the   further

            more

leaf
  speak

  fertility
   in

  parent
he
   ses

branches as if the allusion is moving between branches

early wind   propped open
                  with a pinecone

a discussion about chromosomes a void in autumn

passes toward an established branch eating into

after the
punch

line
the head

line
branches

again the
    patriotic

song
breaks

down
    in

to
  laughter

              glass wind bears
                across thinning war
                    faces

full of inversion
anxiety   age
of an idiom
opening

carries his seashore wears his coat to distant teeth

a hymn out
night's mute
housestain

fully opened
the her within
cherry

man

U

fact

U

red
rose

echoing mountain
lingering body

not hearing the c
in crib a
wintry crust

breast veins more pronounced hummingbird

so usually she's whatever the branches are saying

anniversary
    an ice cream flavor
    named Terrorism

revenge apple with a larger genome

sleep
walking
                        spring

                    sea
    a
new
    born

        near

: thunder obeying,

the violet.

. She became the

unload
ed bells

drifts of
her

face

long
points

of
snow

am

n   i

                              o
              tic

     flu
id
     winter

                         stars

        do not
             just

     wish

        to

                    talk

myths slashed and burned a forest dragged to the sea

the river entering the
sea a sheet of
paper

where it flows through
new laws a woman
gathering

water candles
at the gate of
newborn eyes

mother and child
provide the voices
of the moon

planets fading back into numbers

BEHEADING

green light

an escalation of policy
slivers of night's glass
slipper

rusty stump
the lichen detaches
from the alphabet

after giving birth
she splits
some logs

                              in her

                           milk
today

                        mushrooms

                              that
                        listened
                              to o

                     ur laughter

at the edge of the sea
a box of my teeth has found me
on a cold day

the first word now without leaves the other wears a condom

radioactive honey
radioactive foxes
radioactive tombs

the dead violet
my lungs continue
to grow from

while reciting
the alphabet
summer arrives

glitter
    covering up
    all
the apostrophes

her theory about me
the wet side
of the mountain

the peach's death is involved smoke

i'm not sure, but it begins with the description of a penny

                                        where seeds
                                        meet sea blacked out
                                        names and phrases

wait, so she never did find out her mother was a robot

wild apple
smells like my
child now

the spider i talk to the spider she talks to

                    invasive species
                cut and left
                    inside nouns

in the seconds between wars frog

we wrote an apology letter to the daffodils of all things

supermarket
veteran

pretends
to shoot

my
daughter

smiling

while we're holding each other i have to move the eggs

her kiss crinkles all the snacks

the pineapple kept falling over so we ate it

her milk
from the back of the freezer
new year's eve

gull
       s settling

around
   us

                    ashes

   from

            a
         different
            fire

new year's eve
we only use
our fingers

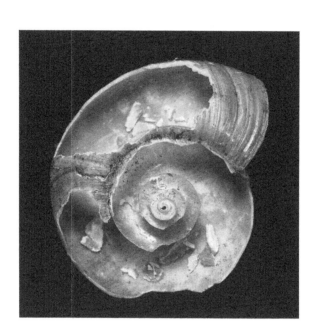

corp
orate
contami
nation

a whale
spouts

far
off shore

unarranged
small plates
new year's day

answers appear questions remain the ocean's cancer wings expand

the
sea

stars
are

almost g
one

in her
hand

a sea

beside
the
cricket

not a
cricket

beside
the sea

between my child and i
corporate language
disguised as a gull

o and by the waves who's we

star

 fish

end

of
 each

whisper

new year's eve a beach fire we inherit and abandon

as a window to
a window of
as father seen

bud breaks now
wider than
our words

        cherry blossom
    flavored
            hyper-violence

her decision all the skin
peeled away from
the flesh of a peach

how the deer's taken
on the valley
colors

death of a friend i also push away the vegetables

surrounded by sharks
the scars
on a child's face

the milky way   an afterthought
   a hand

ful of

        warm
     sea   snail

              shells

do you imagine it's one frog or more than   one   how

about

now

a void in

g the crystallized violence

Cherry Petals

cherry
blossoms
clear

brow

ser

his
story

o she barely whispered stars

path s thr ugh the w ld flow rs

. At
her. B
est.

th. Is a
nd. Th
. At

. For the
ir. Nes
t. S

alone
with
her

pine
cone
double

speak

at some
point a berry
was bound
to speak
to her

(cracked	40
fingertips	Lake,
cherry	Yellow
stained)	6
Red	Lake

the insect that pinches at the center of the night peach

like i threw nothing out
the door
    the dandelion seed

like Dracula
Whitman came in
with the cat

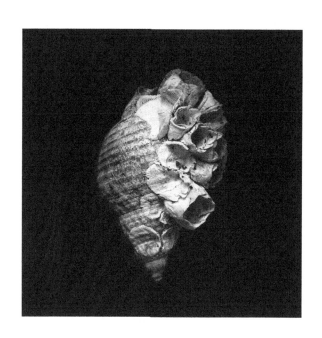

is the
ocean
                    the
                    ocean
still
                    still
there
is
                    there

she
asks
if
           from
these
foot
prints
           years
are
mine
           ago

must
have

        some
        thing
        like

moon
light

        a

year's
first

        nurse

        ry rhy

dream

        me

BREAKFAST ALL DAY
the cereal called *Fear Mongering*
comes with a free toy

be
tween
                    (*in*

ma   (*a*
le
af f
all
                    the

s) ss s
hoot
ings
                    pond)

. Violence in   every

"New World"   i go   bare

        foot.   . In the sand—

her glass eye missing woman washed ashore

the two languages of warming a stone with my fingers

listen
ing to
her

what
might
be

watch
ing

a
distant
boat

ring

finger

symbols

in
the

shore
line
pull
of
her tiny hand

a deer. On   . The beach,

kind   of

, tidepool,

a fire to   , "Watch it

fade.   Fade.   . The first rain

, in ash,   . In   . The wine

she
calls
         this
         universe
the
         wing
glass
         ing
ice
         it

the napkin with an insect wing inside it unfolds

mostly footnotes
today mostly footnotes
about the rain

my child talks to my shadow too many leaves

                    she
                       crawls
                     out

                    of a
                    laugh

                    explores
                    the spot

                    where

                        a

                    butterfly

                      was

If   , if   (daffodils)

          stay   . There—

          All day,

waters

                    the
                    stone

                    waters

         the
         butterfly

         waters

                    the
                    water

swept up old
nails skin cooked
separately

elk carcass
      plans for next year
   carved into the bones

her long conversation with the moon ends with the word funny

Look — Inside — Her curled
dreaming Shell — a loved Copy —
of — Wonder — Land —

since she   , wore m

y grandmother's perfume   i   , lingered,

—deep into   . Dusk.

for
some
                    work

un
known

                    just
                    the

reason

                    sound

a
fire

                    far
                    away

. A coat   that, no

        longer.   fits   . A town

that, no   longerspeaks

                    wear
                    condoms

our   burn
words   neon

                    want
                    spring

she fans herself between her legs songs the birds make after singing the plastic covering the moon loosens

feast day half Rockwell half Dali

                                    family
        laughter

        through
        the stained   glass

        basement
         window

                    of
                                        falling

                    snow

convince. D

. It

wanted.

Her

, to catch,

it.

. We

. Speak

of them.

as   .

. They were

one.

of us.

too deep a breath not deep enough cherry blossom

sometimes the sea laughs in its sleeping child

. After i
said, "That

                    sh. E
asked. If she
        . "Could
become.

. Pre
        g. N
            ant.

    from. Hold
in. G

        . A
    humming. B
            ir. D

Then —
Other —
  butterflies joined — her & — The Butterfly — The End —

words

        from

no

one

        the

        clown

        s

s

p

ends

time

        on

        the

with

away

        screen

        s

dad, the sea's within

reach

        dad

they're
planting
some

              one
in the
grave

        yard

dad

          a child's gift shop
       in the belly
          of a dune

from
  a distance

i watch
her

lips
  moving

whales

  along
the shore

all the acorns taken out to sea float back into her hands

        one

        bird
        note."

        she i
        mitates

        one

        bird
        note."

easier to write
about birds and flowers than
hands and knees on necks

                              law and
                              order

                              being

                              tossed
                              around

                              all the
                              leaves

                              turning

                              alter

                              native
                              shades

we've eaten all the mushrooms that chose us all souls' day

feast day room left for riots

an inflated Santa
on a military police truck
waving to an empty lot

a neurological season
so we believe
        in neurological seasons

how. It stands
by windows. And doors and broken
people. By flags

a
scream
a flag
still
as a
statue

the mountainside blooms terrorists like you wouldn't believe

the empty streets of little coughs little sneezes little looks the virus we

lean

so many
things
against

the cherry
tree

my next god is open peony's shadow

a new

god's
logo

al
ready al
tered

summer
winds

with a candle i go all the way into her line about spring

summer wind
crawls back
into its shell

all
that

for

a
leaf

. Pharma
cy.
                    door
                    opened
   . By
the wind opened

by the
rain

a neighbor's scent has changed winter fog

first

        then

she's

        a blue

a blue
sky's
mask

        sky's
        ghost

in the back of a drawer
balled up pages
from Wonderland

eyelashes on the introduction

the virus again the child wants to see what it looks like

rain

lull

a
by

rain

lull

a
b

y i
L u
V U

the window left open in a dancing position she fell asleep

enough moonlight
on the beach
to build a scarecrow

our voices shift the sea and i trade masks

until it's cleared
by the machine
summer sky

firefly

   memories

passing
  through

  the
   skin
 of
  another

  galaxy

we speak more
through this
back window

through mountains
that were once people
fireflies

a boy

dressed
as a

skeleton
dances

on the
beach

moss covered stones when we're shown open doors in the creek

summer left behind
marks that look
like moths

after washing vegetables
she opens up
all of the windows

sweet potatoes
roasting in the embers
of old furniture

everyone's asleep early and everyone's covered in that light

a stone

gently

turned

even
older

gods

standing in the creek some planets are only made of gas

mountains on the other side of her fireflies

creek mouth the ribs of a myth

                              star
                               to

                                 star

                              the
                              web

                                rebuilt

                                 over

                              night

some decorations out in this part of keep out private property

the new masks behind the new masks

once we were distant boat lights lighting up new year's day

a cold day
of short conversations
with machines

i think she said her last meal was snowflakes

anyway it *looked* like a leaf and it *spoke* like a leaf

no
   word

yet
  what

kind
 of

   window

 it
should
  be

in the scratch in the mirror the leg of an insect

butterflies bring out the prophet in her

we talk to the shell
that's been talking
to the moon

a mask that took
all morning

replaced by
the mask

that took
all night

cockroaches
nonetheless
militarized

new device
a new god
speaks of a garden

church parking lot
air conditioning
from an open door

ants
looking for apple blossoms
inside the apple

steps laughed at by the sea

most of their discography while the mushrooms dry

new year's day
she throws away
her own milk

sounds people usually make winter rain

like early streetlights
in a small town museum
beached jellyfish

mask to mask the sea and i

shot
through

the machine
washed

a
shore

pecked
away

breeze
by breeze

corporate merger
the sea anemone's mouth
is also its anus

shaped by the sea shaped by the rain child's hunger

suck
in

the
seconds

between

winter   stars
fish
in
g

boat

lights

the list of
possible

side
effects

sewn
together

into a
mask

it gallops along so much for cherry blossoms

.

               under

water

               budding

branches

               similes

touch

and
 go

playing all the parts
hand upon
earth

eat ng h les as th y cro s the sky ast r sks

a firefly
mask

a language
slowly

being

born

it's hard to find a limb for them

a virus
          shaped
          day

          a
               thunder

                    bird
     shaped
night

wind inter mourn in a wake end by a diction airy

winter
              dusk
              is a
coldness
              a rock
from
the beach
              in my
              palm
is a
coldness

morning's door
i am pushed open by
a crooked flower

i looked everywhere outside except the first sentence

around
 the cracked

mirror
 hooks

. "For the

w. ln d

rain
 masks

dolls

trillium

another

spring

light

pulled
through

side effects include hummingbirds just before dawn a heartbeat

we fast. Forward
ed then rewound. Through
The genocide

the butterfly. Just
going along. Resurrecting
this. That

"Well, I guess
"Summer's
"Been
"A simple
song
"From a
broken
"Computer

a drug store replaced
a car dealership you say
you can hear the sea now

a plastic. Bottle

of water. Gently

                washed.
With

    . A plastic

        bottle. Of

water.

hands
  upon
  breasts

leaves
  upon
  creek

  stones

the pine needle it took years away

scare. Crow

's in.

vest.

ment.

port.

folio.

. Stick

ing through.

. Its

. Head

all the windows open you know the house next to the cemetery

snow. Skin

peeled. From a

. Bar

. Code

night.

until his words become nothing familiar leaves up and gone

yes that flower opens
every door
in the house

she can. Only

take. So, many

butter.

flies.

hitting.

The wind.

. Shield

dunno
maybe

                they go

            under
              ground

        to get
        away

            from
            the
                flowers
                and
                all

            the
            nonsense

all the doors all the windows summer heartbeats double checked

rusted fogline
a piece of plastic
in each talon

a small
round
window
                    spoken
                    of
                            as

                    the

                        sea
opens
  up   a few
                hands
    a few
    eyes

but it's
still

just   as
one
ocean
                     happens
waving
                     in
                     stars

. We both

—mention

. While

, undressing,

. The scent of the

, peaches,

. In

. The Other

room

a day of negotiations
with the cats
and the sea

5   chldrn

    inthe   ap
               ple

tReee

no more crow fall's highway

solstice passing around her now their dictionary complete

heblames

the
  m asks

    . For

her
  choices
  his

h and

writ in g

bro ken

m ntain

r ange

that day

 once
again

               when
the sea is

 full of
              bruised

              and
              bitten
apples

win. Ter

. Night

.The cat

's skeleton. Has

a few. More

letters.

th.

. An

. The alpha

. Bet

Aphro
dite

Vishnu

Babbitt

washed
up

jellyfish

acidified
sea

certain

gods
        push

sing

pull

echo

cleaning its fur
the night knocks
petals down

there were larger insects and the moon was a little closer

more atomized

bison   lion
women   men

frayed   empire
edges

. Ga

   . La

xy.

     . After g

. A

lax. Yo

f. A

     ut. U

mn. Li

   ght. Tr

icks.

     ter. S

we left

their faces
blank

mammoth
bone

home

we
immediately

change

how

the
story
begins

a flower
blooming
from
the
roof

all

the
lies

all

the
tools

in this

house

alone

at first
  the drone

operator
looks

as if
deep in

  prayer

        urnt
    vill ge
        eems to me
      t e
underw rld

Yes, in that state
they might wear
cicada masks.

the virus the smell
of the machine
working overtime

may

flies

another
thou

sand
masks

of
god

s. Had

ow. S

of black.

. Bi

rd. S

mo. Ve

b. Lack b

irds. M

oved. By

th. E

. Cree

k.

on the prepositions under the leaf's verbs

                some
                of   the
                                      leaves

                                      really
                                          get
                you

below

the
falls

a
glass

bottom

boat
  drifts

      into
dharma

    shadows

until   it was

. "Only,

        you

                realize

th. E
sound.
  —of

the
rain

      , dripping,

               from.
              . Every
               thing

muddy
paw   prints   a
                cross   the
                    night's wind
                              shield

. In

. So far

                    . As
                , birds,

        . Are

    concer

            ne. D

takes

leaves

of

its

light

bird. S
, after
all,
. That

. Birds
after.
. All

. *That*

so
i guess

we're
a lot

like
leaves

her garden won't quit

a leaf remembered a mountain forgotten

                                        eating
                                        the odor

                                        of burning
                                        trees

                                        the other

                                                edge

                                        of land

. Fa

ll

. lng

. Le

aves.

. Wo

rds.

. Un   rea. D

. Un

fini

shed.

fire

        and
wind   parables

leaves

        also
talk

        with
        their
        hands

Anthropocene. Who is
that. Standing by
        the stage. Door

Acknowledgments

I would like to thank the following people for their generous time and thoughts in helping me put this collection together: Cherie Hunter Day, Chris Gordon, Richard Gilbert, Lee Gurga, Jim Kacian, Eve Luckring, Paul Pfleuger, Jr., and Peter Yovu. And for their love and friendship, thank you to my parents, Jeff, Jason, Rob, and John.

Some of the poems in this collection first appeared, sometimes in different forms, in the following publications: *Acorn, ant ant ant ant ant, Bones: journal for the short verse, bottle rockets, CLWN WR, frogpond, Heliosparrow Poetry Journal, Hummingbird, Kingfisher Journal, is/let, MASKS, Modern Haiku, NOON: journal of the short poem, NOON: an anthology, One Sentence Poems, otata, Otoliths, Presence, Roadrunner, Right Hand Pointing, The Heron's Nest, Under the Bashō, Whiptail.* My thanks to the editors of these journals and magazines.

AUTHOR'S NOTE

SCOTT METZ is a poet living on the central Oregon coast, the traditional homelands of the Alsea, Siletz, Tillamook, and Yakina peoples. His first collection of poems, *lakes & now wolves*, was published by Modern Haiku Press in 2012. He has been an editor for the online journals *is/ let, MASKS*, and *Roadrunner*, and coeditor, with Lee Gurga, of *Haiku 21* along with a string of yearly anthologies, all for Modern Haiku Press. His poems have been featured in *The Disjunctive Dragonfly* by Richard Gilbert (Red Moon Press, 2013), and *Haiku in English: The First Hundred Years* (W. W. Norton, 2013; eds. Burns, Kacian & Rowland).